I CAN BE...

ELLYSE PERRY

From city kid to Aussie legend

Published by Affirm Press in 2015
28 Thistlethwaite Street, South Melbourne, VIC 3205
www.affirmpress.com.au

With thanks to Cricket Australia

Visit www.throwhitcatch.com.au
www.playcricket.com.au

National Library of Australia Cataloguing-in-Publication entry available for this title at www.nla.gov.au.
Title: I Can Be ... Ellyse Perry/ Phil Kettle, author.
ISBN: 9781925344097

Cover illustrations by David Dunstan
Cover design by Karen van Wieringen
Typeset in Noteworthy 14.5/24pt and Georgia 14.5/24
All cartoons by David Dunstan, design by Karen van Wieringen

Proudly printed in Australia by Griffin Press

FSC www.fsc.org MIX Paper from responsible sources FSC® C009448

The paper this book is printed on is certified against the Forest Stewardship Council® Standards. Griffin Press holds FSC chain of custody certification SGS-COC-005088. FSC promotes environmentally responsible, socially beneficial and economically viable management of the world's forests.

Phil Kettle

Illustrations by David Dunstan

I CAN BE... ELLYSE PERRY

From city kid to Aussie legend

Affirm press

CRICKET AUSTRALIA

Under the Southern Cross I stand
A sprig of wattle in my hand,
A native of my native land,
Australia, you little beauty.

INTRODUCTION

I've really got to be one of the luckiest people in the entire world.

Just imagine: me, Jill King, ten years old, living at Mistake Creek in outback Queensland, being invited by Cricket Australia to meet my cricket heroes.

When my next-door neighbour, Jack Ace, said we should write to Cricket Australia and ask if we could meet some famous cricketers, we never thought we'd ever hear from them.

Fortunately, we were wrong. Not only did Cricket Australia contact us, they arranged for us to come to the National Cricket Centre in Brisbane to meet some legends of the game.

Ms Rowles, our school principal, agreed to allow us to take time off school, as long as we wrote a report on each of the cricketers we met.

I would like to thank **Greg Chappell** and **Belinda Clark**, who are cricketing legends, for their help and assistance.

She bats. She bowls. She can defend and kick goals. **Ellyse Perry's** achievements are unique in Australian sport.

CHAPTER ONE

An all-rounder

JiLL: I'm very pleased to meet you, Ellyse. You really are a superstar sports person!

Ellyse: And I'm pleased to meet you, Jill. I'm not sure that I'm a superstar sports person, though. I really just try to be the best that I can be.

JiLL: Well, I think you're a superstar. I also think that most Australians think you're a superstar. Anyone who has represented Australia in soccer – or, as the fans call it, football – ***and*** cricket has to be a superstar!

Ellyse: There has certainly been a lot of hard work to get to where I am, not only by me, but by my family who have supported me, as well.

JiLL: Is it true that you represented Australia in both cricket and football in the same year – and you were only 16?

Ellyse: Yes, that's true.

Jill: Wow! Well, today we're going to be talking about cricket mostly, but before we do, I want to ask you one question about football. Has playing football made you a better cricketer?

Ellyse: I think that playing lots of different sports helps you to improve your skills in every sport that you play. Playing football certainly helped improve my fitness and footwork, which, in turn, has helped improve my cricket.

QLD
NSW
SYDNEY
VIC

CHAPTER TWO

From the start

JiLL: Tell me about where you grew up.

Ellyse: I was born in the Sydney suburb of Wahroonga. I lived in a house with my mum, dad and older brother.

JiLL: Wow, Sydney! That's a big city. My town, Mistake Creek, is only small, but there's plenty of space to play cricket. Do you think that growing up in the city meant you couldn't play as much as someone from the country?

Ellyse: No, not at all. I was always able to play with my family, and there were lots of opportunities to do sport at school.

JILL: What schools did you attend?

Ellyse: I attended Beecroft Public School. Then I went to Pymble Ladies' College.

JILL: My favourite subject at school is sport. Did you like sport at school, too?

Ellyse: Yes! I was sports captain, athletics captain and cricket captain.

JILL: So your favourite school subject was sport, as well!

Ellyse: Yeah, I'm pretty sure there wasn't any other subject that I liked as much as I liked sport.

JILL: Did you do anything extraordinary when you were growing up?

Ellyse: I think I was just like everybody else. I went to school. I had lots of friends. I spent my weekends either playing sport or at the beach.

JILL: Were you always good at sport?

Ellyse: I think I was good at sport, but I also really loved competing. That made a difference to my motivation, I think.

CHAPTER THREE

The backyard

JILL: What got you interested in sport?

Ellyse: My family.

JILL: My family helped me get interested in sport, as well. Every time I go inside the house, my mum and dad tell me to go outside and play. The only person I can play with is Jack. Jack is actually the only other kid who lives near me in Mistake Creek.

Ellyse: So, Jack likes sport, too?

JILL: He loves sport. He always says if you can't hit it, throw it or kick it, it's not worth talking about.

Ellyse: Did Jack get you interested in sport?

JILL: He certainly did! It didn't take long before I realised I could hit, throw and kick every bit as good as Jack! Sometimes even better!

Ellyse: Growing up, I don't think I had any choice other than to be interested in sport. My family is a sports-crazy family.

JiLL: What sports do you all play?

Ellyse: A whole range of sports! My mother is a former swimmer. My father played cricket and squash at representative level, and my brother, Damien, loves cricket. Sport has always been important in our house. I was encouraged to give all sports a go, and that's just what I did.

JiLL: It seems that you must have excelled at two of the many sports you tried, since you've represented Australia in football and cricket!

SWIMMING
PERRY
1st
PERRY
PERRY
PERRY

Ellyse: Yes, I guess that was the case!

Jill: What do you think first made you interested in the great game of cricket?

Ellyse: Watching my dad teach Damien to bowl was what made me interested in cricket.

Jill: What did you learn from watching?

Ellyse: Mostly, that I wanted to try to play! I'm not really a watching type of person. I'd much rather be part of the action.

JiLL: Why watch when you can play? That's what I say!

Ellyse: That's good advice. If more people did that, then more people would be playing sport, and that'd be really good for everyone.

JiLL: So, when your dad was coaching your brother, did you ask if you could practise, too?

Ellyse: Yes. I didn't know it at the time, but you could say my backyard served as my sporting apprenticeship. My father taught me to bowl, but it was actually my brother who improved my bowling.

JILL: How did he do that?

Ellyse: My brother found new ways to interpret the rules of cricket, which meant it was nearly impossible for me to get him out!

JILL: So, that meant you spent a lot of time bowling, so you were able to improve. Interesting ... Can you put me in touch with Damien?

Ellyse: Uh, why would you want to contact my brother, Jill?

JILL: I want to get a copy of his rulebook. I could use it when I play against Jack!

Ellyse: It might improve Jack's bowling, though!

JILL: I hadn't thought of that. It seems to me the backyard has played an important part in the development of most successful cricketers.

Ellyse: That's for sure. The backyard, the park, a bit of flat ground anywhere, plus a couple of rubbish bins, a bat and a ball, and you can start working your way towards playing for Australia!

CHAPTER FOUR

From the backyard to the cricket park

JiLL: When did you first start playing in a cricket team?

Ellyse: I started playing in a boys' team when I was at primary school.

JiLL: How hard was it playing against the boys?

Ellyse: I never thought much about the fact that I was playing against boys. To me, they were just other kids playing the same game that I loved playing. Plus, my older brother had always treated me just like anyone else when it came to playing in the backyard.

JILL: When did you first play in a girls' team?

Ellyse: I made the local regional girls' cricket team, and from there, I was picked in the NSW state primary schools' team.

JiLL: Was that the start of you thinking that, one day, you might play for Australia?

Ellyse: I don't remember ever thinking about playing for Australia when I was in primary school. I was just keen to make as many representative teams as I could.

JiLL: You certainly did that, because at the age of 16, you were playing first for New South Wales, and then for Australia!

Ellyse: I guess I was a bit lucky.

JiLL: I don't think luck has much to do with it when you get selected to play for Australia.

Ellyse: There sometimes can be a little bit of luck.

JiLL: Like when?

Ellyse: Performing well, when it counts.

JiLL: Jack told me something that Greg Chappell said: 'the harder you work, the luckier you will be.'

Ellyse: I'm pretty sure that my dad thinks the same way. He made me work hard at my sport, but at the same time, he always said that it had to be fun.

JiLL: Who has been the most important person in your sporting development?

Ellyse: That's easy to answer. My dad has been, and still is, the most important person in my sporting career.

JiLL: Maybe we all need to have someone to help guide us sometimes. My granddad has helped me.

Ellyse: How has he done that?

JiLL: My granddad, Alf Gates, is a total legend in Mistake Creek. Our town plays an annual cricket match against Springsure. My grandfather is the captain and the team's star player. Rumour has it that one year, he hit six sixes in one over. The last six he hit went so far that the ball landed in a crow's nest ... five kilometres from the oval! Granddad always tells me that I should play with determination and a smile on my face.

Ellyse: That's really good advice. Being determined is important, and having a smile on your face is also really good. Sometimes it's not that easy to do, but it's important to keep a positive attitude as much as you can.

Jill: Yeah. Sometimes, when Jack bowls me out, I do find it hard to keep smiling ...

AUSTRALIA

CHAPTER FIVE

Australia and more

JiLL: How excited were you when you were selected to play for Australia for the first time?

Ellyse: On a scale of one to ten, I'd say it was about a 13!

JiLL: What did it feel like when you walked out onto the playing arena for the first time with your new teammates?

Ellyse: I thought I would be nervous, but I wasn't. I was incredibly excited and looking forward to the contest.

Jill: I guess that's part of what makes you a champion.

Ellyse: I think I'm a long way off being a champion! I always feel like there's more I can do to develop as a player.

Jill: But you're one of the best players in the world! Even though you are a lot older than me, you're still young. Do you think you will keep improving as a player?

Ellyse: The day I don't think that I can improve anymore will be the day that I know I've reached my peak. That's when I'll be ready for my cricket career to come to an end.

JILL: I definitely hope that you keep improving for a very long time, and I'm sure all other Australians do too, so we can keep watching you play.

Ellyse: So do I.

JiLL: Have you got any advice for girls, no matter where they live, who want to play cricket?

Ellyse: Just pick up a bat or ball and join in! In cricket, it doesn't actually matter whether you're a boy or a girl. Cricket is a game that everyone can play.

JiLL: What's the best thing about cricket?

Ellyse: I think the best thing about cricket is that it's a team game. The bonds that develop between you and your teammates from playing together last forever.

JiLL: There seems to be a lot of exciting things happening in women's cricket.

Ellyse: Women's cricket is going through a very exciting growth period. We have the Big Bash League starting soon, along with lots of other world tournaments. I'm really excited.

JILL: Do you think there's a chance that I can play in your team in the Big Bash?

Ellyse: I'll certainly tell the selectors that you're available.

JILL: Thank you for allowing me to spend some time with you. I'm sure that there are girls all over Australia who have read this and are saying, 'I can be Ellyse Perry!'

Ellyse: Thank you, Jill! It's been a pleasure.

WBBL
WBBL

MS
ROWLES

RESEARCH

Before we left school to go to the National Cricket Centre, Ms Rowles said we could get out of class, but only on one condition.

'I want the kids who read your stories to understand what has made each of the cricketers you meet the champion players they are,' she said. 'I want facts, tips and information about them. Anything that will help your readers have a better understanding of cricket. You have to research,' she said. And then she repeated the word 'research' for emphasis.

When Ms Rowles tells you to do something, that's what you do … of course!

The first thing I needed to do was find out what exactly 'research' means.

RESEARCH: An investigation into a specific subject so you can find out more about it.

If there's one thing Jack and I like nearly as much as cricket, it's investigating, so we took to it like a ferret after a rabbit.

FACTFILE

Ellyse Alexandra Perry (born 3 November 1990) is an Australian sportswoman. She plays for the Australian women's cricket team and the New South Wales women's cricket team.

Ellyse made her debut for both the Australian cricket and football teams at the age of 16.

Ellyse played her first international cricket match in July 2007. She earned her first football cap for Australia just one month later!

Ellyse is the youngest person to represent Australia in cricket.

Ellyse is also the first Australian to have appeared in both cricket and football World Cups.

Ellyse is ranked in the top ten batters and bowlers in One Day International women's cricket.

WOMEN'S CRICKET

Dad thinks girls playing cricket must be something that has only happened in recent times. I found that hard to believe, knowing what a great game cricket is. I thought girls would have always wanted to play cricket! History is one of my favourite subjects at school, so I decided that I needed to find out more about the history of women's cricket. I've got to tell you, what I found out surprised me!

- The first recorded women's cricket match was played on the 26 July 1745!

- In Australia, a women's cricket league was set up in 1894.

- The first international women's cricket Test match was played between England and Australia in December 1934.

- About 247,000 women play cricket. That's heaps! And females make up 22 per cent of the total number of people who play cricket in Australia.

THE AUSTRALIAN WOMEN'S NATIONAL CRICKET LEAGUE

Did you know that the Women's National Cricket League (WNCL) is the national competition for women's cricket in Australia?

I also learnt that there are six domestic women's teams. In the league competition, the six teams play each other in two 50-over matches. The side that has won the most matches after the preliminary rounds then hosts the finals series. The finals are 'best-out-of-three'.

The first WNCL took place in the summer over 1996–97. It replaced the Australian Women's Cricket Championships, which had taken place in a two-week tournament format for the previous 66 years.

A Twenty20 competition was also introduced for the domestic teams in the 2008–09 season, and ACT and Tasmania joined in the following season.

I'm really enjoying learning more about cricket through research. I think I like research almost as much as I like cricket! Maybe when I grow up, I can be a cricketer and a researcher.

Do you want to try out your research skills? I have a challenge for you! Try to find out:

- which Australian states have teams?
- what are the team names?
- what colours are each team's uniforms?

You can find the answers by visiting **www.throwhitcatch.com.au**

ONE DAY INTERNATIONAL (ODI)

There are different formats of our great game of cricket, including Test matches, One Day games and Twenty20 games. The rules for each format are different.

In One Day International matches, two international teams play against in other. That means it's the best of the best! The usual rules are used in these matches, except that each team only gets to bat a fixed number of overs.

It's usually 50 overs. Because of this, ODIs are also called Limited Overs Internationals.

FIELDING RESTRICTIONS AND POWER-PLAYS

In an ODI, there are a limited number of fielders allowed in the outfield during power-plays. These are called 'fielding restrictions'.

Fielding restrictions change during the game, so there are a different amount of fielders allowed in the 30-yard circle depending on the over.

In the first ten overs, there can only be two fielders outside the 30-yard circle

Between 11 to 40 overs, four fielders are allowed outside to field there.

In the final ten overs, five fielders are allowed to field outside the 30-yard circle.

I've discovered how many overs each team can face, but I've left out the number of overs a bowler can bowl. Can you find the answer?

To check if you're right, go to
www.throwhitcatch.com.au

SCORE 102
WKTS 7
OVERS 31

BATTING AVERAGES

In cricket, a player's batting average is the total number of runs he or she has scored divided by the number of times he or she has been out.

In the last five backyard Test matches that I've played against Jack's team, I've scored:

55 not out

67 not out

33 out

52 out

107 not out

Can you work out my batting average?

TOTAL RUNS ÷ TIMES OUT

You can check your answer by visiting
www.throwhitcatch.com.au

I know that my batting average is good, but did you know that Sir Donald Bradman has the highest batting average in the entire history of Test cricket?

What do you think his average is?

You can perform some of your own research, and then check your answer at **www.throwhitcatch.com.au**

AUSTRALIAN CRICKET GROUNDS

The SCG

Australia has some of the best cricket grounds in the world! One of these is the Sydney Cricket Ground, or SCG.

The SCG is a sports stadium in Sydney, in case you couldn't guess by its name. It was first established in 1854, and the first cricket Test match played in it was against England in 1882. Today, it is used for Test cricket, One Day International cricket and Twenty20 cricket, as well as AFL and some rugby league and rugby union matches. It can seat 48,000 people!

The SCG is the home ground for the New South Wales Blues cricket team and the Sydney Sixers in the Big Bash League.

You can find out more about the SCG by visiting

www.sydneycricketground.com.au

MISTAKE CREEK

BOWLING IN MISTAKE CREEK

Did you know that Mistake Creek is where backyard swing bowling was invented? Really, I'm telling the truth! Well, at least I think that it's the truth.

My grandfather, when he was a boy – and that was so long ago that electricity hadn't even been invented – decided that he wanted to become a champion cricketer.

To help with this dream, he decided that he was going to make a cricket wicket in his backyard.

As we all know, a cricket pitch is 22 yards (or 20.12 metres) long.

Now, the problem my grandfather had was this: no matter how hard he tried, he couldn't find a space that was long enough to make a pitch. Along one side fence was the chook shed. Along the other side fence was the laundry, and in front of the back fence was a work shed. To make matters worse, in the middle of the yard was a big tree.

Granddad thought about cutting the tree down, but after telling his mother (my great-grandmother) of his plans, he was informed that his life wouldn't be worth living if he went anywhere near it with the axe.

It just so happened that right when he thought there was no way that he was going to have a wicket in his backyard, he had a dream. He dreamt about a ball that, when bowled, would swing through the air, bending like a banana.

The next morning, Granddad was very excited, because he knew just what to do. He was going to have a cricket wicket in his backyard.

He mowed, he rolled, he marked out the wicket, and he put stumps in at both ends of the pitch.

When he had finished, he smiled, admiring what he'd achieved.

My granddad invited his two best friends around to play cricket. But when they arrived, they looked at the wicket and laughed.

'How can we play cricket on this wicket? There's a tree in the middle of the pitch!' they both said at the same time.

Granddad explained to his friends about his dream, and how it had led him to invent the very first swinging backyard cricket ball.

'What I've done is taken this tennis ball and taped up one side. Now, because the taped side is heavier than the other side of the ball, it will swing through the air, which will allow it to bend around the tree,' my grandfather explained.

Still not convinced, one of his friends took his bat and went to the batter's end.

Granddad bowled the ball. Not only did it swing around the tree, it clean bowled his friend! And that is how the backyard swinging cricket ball was invented.

(It's possible that I might need to do some more research to make sure that this is a true story ...)

CRICKET TERMS

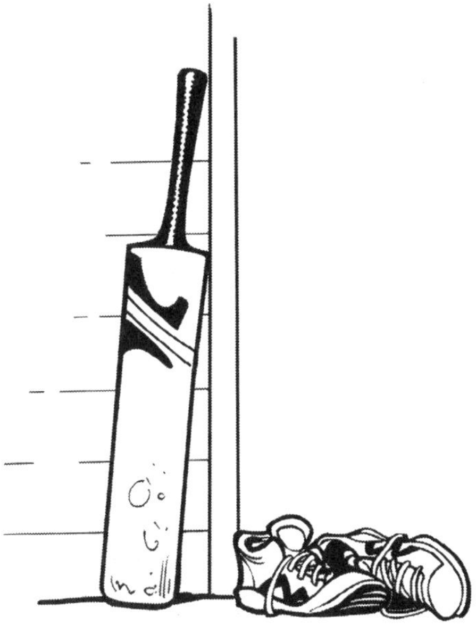

Jack and I are learning so much about cricket from doing all this research. I hope you are, as well! Do you know the meaning of these cricket terms? If you're not sure, you can practise your research skills, too.

Clean bowled:

Dot ball:

Duck:

Economy:

Drive:

Edge:

Extras:

Farm the strike:

Draw: ______________________________

____

____

Featherbed: ______________________________

____

____

Fence: ______________________________

____

____

Find the answers

www.throwhitcatch.com.au

ELLYSE'S OTHER PASSION

The McGrath Foundation

Ellyse's charity of choice is the McGrath Foundation.

Jane and Glenn McGrath's much-publicised experience with breast cancer led to the formation of one of Australia's most respected and recognised charities, the McGrath Foundation.

The McGraths believed that every family experiencing breast cancer in Australia should have access to the support of a breast care nurse. This shaped the McGrath Foundation's mission to ensure that women can access breast care nurses, no matter where they live or their financial situation.

The McGrath Foundation is considered to be one of Australia's leading breast cancer support organisations, with over 33,000 Australian families supported by 102 McGrath breast care nurses nationally in the past six years.

The Foundation is working to increase breast cancer awareness right across the community to ensure that young Australian women are well-informed about their bodies and can remain in the best health possible.

www.mcgrathfoundation.com.au

BOOKS IN HOMES AUSTRALIA

Jack and I think we are pretty lucky. We live in a fantastic town. We go to a great school. We live in nice homes. We have great parents and, thankfully, our homes have lots of books. I really love books and reading. The truth is, the more you read, the smarter you get!

Reading has also helped me do the research for these cricket books.